A DOG FIGHT, WITH A JUNKYARD DOG:
Defending Against the Koch/Republican Agenda to Turn America into Nazi Germany

By

Jim Green

DEDICATED TO:

THOSE Democrats who have it going on….who understand they are in a Dog Fight With A Junkyard Dog…who never for a second forget it in our campaigns, and sharpen their teeth on the truism: That the Republican Party, today, is like a wounded animal, striking out in desperation—assorted factions made up of, and taken over by radical extremists, fascists, racists, and the agenda of the Koch Brothers----with the corrupt mind-set that they have license to lie [indistinguishable in intent from the manipulative "Big Lie" in 1930's Germany]----And in their desperation they have no lower limit in their fallacious attacks—which we hear daily on Faux, and radical right radio….With their pernicious racist attacks on President Obama, consummate proof of the above…and include, but are not limited to the 225 Republicans in the House—the 225 certifiable….no chance for recovery ….vapid, idiotic nut job Republicans who voted on 7/30/14, to sue President Obama…..sigh…..

ISBN-13: 978-1500723118

ISBN-10: 1500723118

PROLOGUE

It is not terrorists Americans should be concerned with going forward in the 21st Century, it is the Republican Party…..

The party has been taken over by extremists—radicals—persons devoid of common decency….such as Ted Cruz, the Koch bros., John Boehner, Paul Ryan, et al….

Who have gone to war against women, children, our seniors, our environment, the poor, our grandchildren, ad nauseam ….and who want to roll civilization back to the 8th Century, BC….

For instance, they want American women barefoot, pregnant and in the kitchen, i.e., persons without rights…just look at what they say and vote on…..

They want to prevent women from having contraceptives—so the government can force women to have children--and if they get pregnant, even if they are raped, or if this puts their life in peril, radical Republicans all across America have voted to shut down our clinics—in their attack on women's rights!

To state in a few words the Republicans, today, are NOT DECENT PEOPLE, it is impossible to call oneself a Christian, and not follow his teachings…..and IT IS IMPOSSIBLE TO BE A CHRISTIAN, AND VOTE REPUBLICAN [on Amazon] in short…decent people do not act the way they do…..

It all started with the watershed election in 2010…and has been all downhill since [more on this, herein]….

And as consummate proof of their lack of decency—the Republican controlled House, set as a PRIORITY…..a word that cannot be stressed strongly enough, here—in their War Against Children, once born, by voting to gut our Food Stamp program—the House Republicans set as a PRIORITY, and voted to cut $40 billion out of Food Stamps [gutting the program], so they could give this $40 billion to the Koch brothers [a metaphor, in part].

In short, the Republican Party, today, wants to force women to have children, which they then want to starve to death—so this money can be squandered on PURE GREED, and pander to their racists, which make up 50% of the Republican party today! In the South, the "R" in Republican stands for Racist!

And talk about hypocrisy….if the Republican Party really supported "smaller government" they would rebuke the systematic destruction of women's rights by their radical fringe [which, in fact, IS the Republican Party, today]….by getting the government out of women's, and the rest of our lives!

A government that advocates forcing women to have children, like the Republican Party, today, is the quintessential definition of "Big Government"!

And in corollary attacks on America, one is the Republican Party's systematic destruction of The Voting Rights Act—with bogus voter fraud laws to prevent minorities, students, etc., from voting—and by cutting our hours and places to vote, and they would repeal the 19th Amendment, giving women the right to vote, in a New York Second, if they could get away with it!

Also, medical experts report that 20 million more Americans now have medical insurance because of the ACA, so the only conclusion that can be drawn from the hysterical fear of the ACA by Republicans [who have voted 52 times to demolish it] is that they are petrified that the ACA WILL work, rather than their specious claims that it won't—and WHY, in the name of all that is decent—would Republicans vote to deny healthcare to 20 million Americans? This is the act of scumbags!

The America Republicans envision for Americans, is one unfit for human habitation.....and their agenda is to lie, cheat and rob to get elected, so they can lie, cheat and rob America blind, if elected.....

And if elected, the Republicans in the House have used the American people as a battering ram, to undermine President Obama, as their means to throw red meat to their base....i.e., their racists.......this is their single agenda— they stand for nothing else...as they daily trash America....

Again, the Republican Party, today, poses a far greater danger to Americans, and America, than terrorists!

AND, We need ask ourselves two questions to validate the truth of everything said above:

1] Did the Koch Brothers fund [spend millions] in ads for TV showing youth being subjected to invasive medical procedures—using Uncle Sam as the evil doctor, in an effort to destroy the ACA, i.e., in the Koch Bros agenda to deny healthcare to millions of Americans? And......

2] Did the Republican controlled House vote to strike $40 Billion from our Food Stamp Program [to gut the program], knowing this would deny food to hungry children—[children they insisted be born by their pernicious stand on anti-choice]?

The answer to both, of course, is a resounding YES....and as every decent-minded person on the planet understands: ANY persons who would do this is a SCUMBAG, a CREEP, BOTTOM-FEEDERS....a decent person would NEVER do this....

Too often Democrats soft-peddle their criticism of the evil-doers who have taken over the Republican Party—perhaps a remnant of the "gentlemen's agreement" of bygone years—but the Koch/Republican agenda, today, poses a real and pernicious threat to America's future—and it borders on irresponsible, today, to be remiss—to not expose these evil-does for what they are, and their evil agenda—THUS the title of this book....

As noted, The 2010 election was a watershed moment for America—and has started America down a path from which we may not be able to recover....and we may now be on the symbolic "Fall" side of the "Fall of the Roman Empire"

Historically, the House picks up seats in opposition to the president in an off-year election...but in 2010 it was an avalanche, and this resulted in a nightmare!

The persons who voted for President Obama in 2008, stayed home in droves, while our racists came out in droves…..[given our flawed electronic voting system gave us the correct numbers—more on this ahead]….but the result ushered in a House full of lunatics, and infected our state houses across America, as well!

The election ushered in Greedy Old Prudes [the new face of the GOP]—many who deny evolution….are climate-change deniers, ad nauseam….in elections bought and paid for by the Koch Brothers…who spent tens of millions of dollars to buy our elections!

Further, 2010 was a Census year in which we re-shuffle our congressional districts….and the Republicans gerrymandered our congressional districts to assure that persons unfit to be a Dog Catcher would be in control of America's future…at current count 225 in the House…..for the next 10 years….

In short, the result of the 2010 election was the dumbing down of America…and we handed the mic to Republican idiots and scumbags—persons unfit to hold ANY public office!

And as only one tiny glimpse into this neo-Republican: The Republican Party, as I write, are cheating millions of Americans out of healthcare, SOLELY to undermine President Obama, and curry favor with our racists...to curry favor with the worst of Americans.... and the most pernicious bottom-feeders on the face of the earth!

Why anyone, with even an ounce of decency would vote Republican today, defies rational human thought!

This is not to say, however, that Democrats have clean hands in the trajectory America has currently been set on...albeit, via passivity, rather than intent.....

In 2008, BEFORE the great meltdown [and we were losing 750,000 jobs a month]....the mantra in that election was FIX UNEMPLOYMENT....and when the Democrats failed to do this---particularly, in the narrow window when they had control of the Senate, House, and White House 2008-10—a retaliatory electorate struck back in 2010, and as noted-- The persons who voted for President Obama in 2008, stayed home in droves, while our racists came out in droves!

Yes, it is easy to write all of this off as "partisan" but the result speaks for itself....the record is the verification...

A major thrust in this book, however, in addition to holding the Republican's feet to the fire.....is devoted to HOW DO WE FIX UNEMPLOYMENT? Because, it is asserted, this is fundamental in our turning around our downward spiral—indeed it may be our only path back....

Every year our politicians, the good and the bad, promise full employment—i.e., the promise of job creation if they are elected—and yet, over the past 65 years we have had only one year in which our jobless rate has dipped below 3%....in 1953...And for clarity---even at 3% unemployment we still have around 5 million jobless in America.....[more on this ahead]....

What is not being discussed by either party, however, is that unemployment is a "no one wins" proposition....the jobless lose, and the market loses.....

And, closing out on this issue, here, with a law I crafted--for our friends in Economics, in academe:

> 3% is the zero-sum threshold above which unemployment triggers inflation by diminishing labor training and skills, under-utilizing capital resources, reducing the rate of productivity advance, increasing unit labor costs, and reducing the general supply of goods and services-- and the loss in income to the Market is compounded exponentially with each percentage point of increase in unemployment, above 3%.

People who write have stuff they want to get out—the missives, and miscellany, here, is stuff I want to get out....

A few closing comments in the Prologue—As Oscar Wilde averred "The only truly worthless opinion is an unbiased one"—so bias, agreed— but always in the interest in getting at the larger goal—the truth....

Incidentally, I published my first book on my 78th birthday—and not that I write that fast, or well—the materials were all there for the better part of the past 30 years, give or take, gathering dust—it was just a matter of pulling them together in some order—also, don't believe any book should be over 60 pages, plus/minus—[this book is an exception, of course] i.e., can be read in the crapper--two hours, max--lol—but it seems best summed up by a very astute observer [wish I could recall their name to give credit]: Persons who write do so because they have no choice [it is a compulsion, an addiction..]—they become an "author", however, when people start reading what they have written….

Finally, a note to the reader—the papers and letters are not in sequence, and apologize for redundancy [please look for the nuggets…Thx--lol]—also, if you are a "typo-wonk"—are more concerned with sentence structure, etc., than content—you probably won't like my writing—and you will find a wayward capital letter, here and there, and appearing out of place and used for emphasis—I chalk up to editorial license and tongue-in-cheek, self-effacing humor—so apologies, here—[I seriously support: Take what you do seriously, but never yourself….]….

Just look for content, please….THX

CHAPTER ONE

Editor: NY TIMES

What we can most learn from the Republican Party today is that because something is stupid, that doesn't mean that some people won't do it....

Take "impeachment" for instance—there is absolute zero reason to be talking about impeachment of President Obama....and even less chance of it succeeding....

And yet demagogues and loonies in the Republican Party, like Ted Cruz and Sarah Palin, throw the word around like a juvenile in a drunken stupor…..actually, most juveniles have better sense….

Indeed, the "I" word is called "red meat" for the base—which raises the question, who on earth is this base?

And we can say with absolute certainty, albeit few will admit it, that a percent of the Republican base are racists. They want to impeach President Obama, solely because he is black….

But since most are not forthcoming [and hide behind "it is his policies, not his color"], we can't get an accurate count on the percent—but with the South changing from Blue to Red overnight, following passage of the Civil Rights Act—you do the math….

Further, medical experts report that 20 million more Americans now have medical insurance because of the ACA—

So the only conclusion that can be drawn from the hysterical efforts by Republicans to undermine the ACA [voting 52 times to demolish it] is that they are petrified that the

ACA WILL WORK—AND THEY DON'T WANT PRESIDENT OBAMA TO SUCEED—and are willing to deny healthcare to 20 million Americans—to pander to their racist constituents!

The lesson, here, is very clear—VOTE DEMOCRAT THIS FALL!

Jim Green, Democrat opponent to Lamar Smith, Congress, 2000

CHAPTER TWO

President Obama/Council of Economic Advisers:

THE HISTORY OF HOW WE GOT WHERE WE ARE

Following WW II, President Truman signed into law the [FULL] EMPLOYMENT ACT of 1946, to provide employment for our returning troops.

Ironically, half-way around the world, Australia codified into their law an almost identical Bill, and for the same reason—

Difference is—Australia actually put their law into effect, and over the next 30 years it was intrinsic to employment policy in Australia that "anybody wanting to work should be able to find a job"—and save for a brief recession in 1961/62 their unemployment was 2%, or less. This period is still referred to as their "Golden Age", in Australia.

Unforeseen by either country, however, in the mid-1970's the world economy underwent a major paradigm shift as a result of the colliding forces of automation, globalization, technology, etc., reaching a critical mass—in brief, an adjustment towards modernity—From a perverse perspective, we became victims of our success....

The instability caused by this transition, however, resulted in a malaise, and ushered in the ill-winds of greed-driven neo-liberalism with its indifference to unemployment, and the likes of Thatcher and Reagan—and the menace of this greed-driven agenda was exploded by Bush II, resulting in obscene disparities in wealth that persists, and is the cause of much friction between right and left, to this day.

It also ushered in high and pervasive unemployment throughout our market-driven economies, the OECD—with 6% unemployment in Australia now the norm, and double-digit unemployment common throughout the Eurozone, to this day.

As a result of the "malaise", however, the U.S. took an aggressive, pro-active role in addressing the, above, economic shift—and in 1978 President Carter signed into law one of the most important laws in the 20th Century--an expansion of President Truman's full employment, i.e., Pro-Market 15 USC § 3101-- which "authorizes" the creation of a "reservoir of public employees" at any time our unemployment in America exceeds "3%"—

But in spite of 3% unemployment being the threshold point above which unemployment starts undermining the Market—

And deficit-neutral HR 870/The Neighbor-To-Neighbor Job Creation Act—A federally mandated Social Insurance, owned by our employed, to provide a fund to hire/train our unemployed—

But in spite of these deficit-neutral, Pro-Market solutions—this Law has never been implemented.

FULL EMPLOYMENT IS A PRO-MARKET CONCEPT, Amazon/Kindle

Jim Green, Democrat opponent to Lamar Smith, Congress, 2000

Bio info: http://www.amazon.com/James-L.-Jim-Green/e/B001KHZIMM/ref=ntt_dp_epwbk_0

CHAPTER THREE

THE HISTORY OF HOW WE GOT WHERE WE ARE II:

In the mid-1970's, the colliding forces of automation, technology, globalization, etc., reached a critical mass, in an adjustment towards modernity, resulting in ubiquitous unemployment in the OECD, and has left their leaders conflicted, ever since, regarding the displaced employee—Eurozone unemployment is still in double digits, with Greece and Spain both in excess of 25%, and high youth unemployment a major factor in Arab Spring.

In the U.S., and as a direct response to this major economic shift in the mid-1970's, we took a pro-active role in addressing—and in 1978 President Carter signed into law 15 USC § 3101--which "authorizes" the creation of a "reservoir of public employment" at any time our unemployment rate in America exceeds "3%".

The following year, in 1979, however, and in a panic over Humphrey-Hawkins—our ultra-conservative foundations, with one foot still on the plantation, and desperate to preserve the "market only" job creation concept, embraced a flawed paper by an obscure MIT student, David L. Birch "The Job Generation Process"; and [with lots of cash] they gave his paper biblical importance, and every president since has cited his finding as gospel....

Birch's paper concluded that "small businesses" were the greatest generator of new jobs—problem is, for the purposes of policy-making—it is BS. In a study at Harvard University in 2010, "The Myth of Small Business Job Creation" The research shows "no systematic relationship between firm size and growth." And the research found that small businesses can actually detract from job growth—

In spite of this, Washington struggles, still, to make this antiquated and unworkable notion, work--that is, our policies, to this day, are framed around the pernicious belief that "The market can provide anybody wanting a job, with a job".....it is a FALSE belief—In short, the world has changed, our solutions haven't, and the result has been a disaster, politically as well as otherwise!

And, as well, "Fix the market, and this will fix unemployment", rather than the exact opposite—"Fix unemployment, and this will fix the market"-- is the Republican One and Only job creation solution, to this day!

It would be impossible to still have 6.2% unemployment, as reported in the August 2014 Jobs Report, if we were on the right path [the result is the proof]—and among other problems with this concept--if the market fails, the unemployed are out of luck!

Further, unemployment is a "social" problem we are seeking to address with a highly unstable, incompatible entity: The Market --That is, the last place we should look for a reliable solution to our unemployment crisis is The Market….

And, what apparently isn't clear going forward in our 21st Century, is that an expanding and contracting public workforce is an INDISPENSABLE component to the EFFECTIVE functioning of a modern market economy—i.e., The Humphrey-Hawkins Full Employment Act was dead-on correct in 1978— and provided a "win-win" solution for America—the jobless win, and the Market wins!

The market thrives when we have a robust, employed, consuming workforce, and it is essential to consumer confidence—and overlooked is that HR 1000 [currently in Committee], and the proposed "Neighbor-To-Neighbor Job Creation Act" [hereafter NTN] See: www.Inclusivism.org [both authorized under Humphrey-Hawkins], are deficit-neutral--Pro-Market "win-win" solutions, and to reiterate: The American people win, and capitalism wins—

Please See: THE NEIGHBOR-TO-NEIGHBOR JOB CREATION ACT: Six Months To Full Employment, on Amazon/Kindle

Jim Green, Democrat opponent to Lamar Smith, Congress, 2000

CHAPTER FOUR

Editor: NY TIMES

Historians will rank President Obama in the top 10 of our presidents, maybe the top 5, given that he signed into law the first step towards fixing our horrid "for profit" healthcare system—and which every president since Theodore Roosevelt had tried, but failed to fix.

And where billions were bled off the top to buy bigger yachts—did not go to the healthcare of anyone—and it became a magnet for persons wanting to get rich, rather than cure our ill.

But the reason why we know President Obama will be ranked so high—is because of the absolute hysteria we see in Republicans, today, who try to run him down. And even those who are not racists, are so petrified they would condemn him if he cured them of cancer.

At the post office the other day a fellow senior told me that President Obama had single-handed put 50 million Americans on welfare—and while the absurdity of these whoppers are mind-shattering—and everyday fodder at "agenda, not the news" Faux---it is proof of the hysteria to run President Obama down, in their fact-free world!

On the other end of the continuum, Reagan will be seen by historians as the worst president in American history—until Bush II pushed him out of last place. But unlike President Obama, this is not personal, it is based on a pernicious fraud perpetrated on the American people:

That is, "Suppy-Side Economics"—the fact remains that our deficit was $60 billion when Reagan took over, and was $10 trillion when Bush left—and an economy in shambles—and it has cost an additional $7 trillion to dig out of the hole Reagan and Bush put America in via the Supply Side Fraud!

This is the Fraud [AKA the "fairytale" and it is the Republican One and Only program to this day!]:

Cut taxes for the 1%, they will build factories all across our fair land, and everybody will have a job in the corporation. So what actually happened?

Well, what the 1% didn't stuff in their pockets, or buy a bigger yacht, from this windfall of cash—they built factories alright…in Indonesia, and they hid their profits in the Cayman Islands, so they would not have to pay taxes, and invest in America—and this fraud has resulted in the greatest disparity of wealth in America, in our history!

And it is because of this pernicious fraud, Reagan will be seen by historians as the worst president in American history—until Bush II pushed him out of last place.

The lesson here is: VOTE DEMOCRAT THIS FALL!

See: OUR GREED AND IGNORANCE, on Amazon/Kindle

Jim Green, Democrat candidate for Congress, Dist 21, TX, 2000

CHAPTER FIVE

President Obama/Council of Economic Advisers:

It is really an uncomplicated bit of logic....common sense actually.....when people are not working, they are not buying [the market is diminished by the absence of their buying power]---Thus, FULL EMPLOYMENT IS A PRO-MARKET CONCEPT, Amazon....

But when we think of unemployment, the mind automatically defaults to the plight of the jobless—which it rightfully should, it is quintessential decency....

But by ignoring the damage this as well causes to the market, we let in the bizarre language of the radical-right [who hate people], like "lazy and don't want to work", or communism, socialism, or God forbid "liberal".....and we allow their phobic fixations to lead us down blind alleys, and undermine our finding a solution....

And, where we really got lost is in the pervasive, as well as pernicious BELIEF that the "Market can provide anybody wanting a job, with a job"....it is pernicious because it is FALSE....[and given "automation", alone, this falsehood is compounded daily by our 21st Century economy] .....with the result that our programs to solve unemployment, in America, have been grossly ineffective—

To use a metaphor....if NASA had relied on FALSE information in planning our trip to the Moon....we would never have gotten there....and that is the current plight of our job creation, today--we stand on one foot and then the other, waiting on the market to solve a problem it is INCAPABLE of solving— RATHER than actually solving the problem of unemployment....

Further, and complicating our finding a solution-- is our ignoring an Economic Law:

Short Definition:

3% is the zero-sum threshold above which unemployment starts substantially undermining the Market--and the loss in income to the Market is compounded exponentially with each percentage point of increase in unemployment, above 3%.

In short, unemployment is a "no one wins" proposition—the jobless lose, and the market loses!

And not inconsequential, we have the "legal authorization", on the books [15 USC § 3101], to limit our unemployment rate to "3%", AND pending/proposed legislation, so that at no time going forward should our unemployment exceed "3%"—if we can just get past our fear of the right-wing lunacy that has taken over our political agenda, in America....

HR 1000/THE NEIGHBOR-TO-NEIGHBOR JOB CREATION ACT, Amazon

Jim Green, Democrat opponent to Lamar Smith, Congress, 2000

CHAPTER SIX

The following is borrowed from the Prologue in The Neighbor-To-Neighbor Job Creation Act [hereafter NTN], to explore in detail how we can, in fact, end our unemployment crisis in the U.S., and the OECD, as well…..a big order, agreed…..but unless we open up this dialogue we will never find a solution to what most agree is the most serious social problem facing America today….

"The Neighbor-To-Neighbor Job Creation Act [hereafter NTN] provides us with the legal mechanism to limit our unemployment--so that at no time in the future will our unemployment rate in America exceed 3%. And the perplexing question asked, here, is why didn't we do this years ago?

In a thumbnail, it is a federally mandated Social Insurance, owned by our employed, to provide a fund to hire/train our unemployed.

And without crossing all the t's, and dotting all the i's—[the actual proposed legislation—ready to go into the hopper—is ahead]…the policy cost for this insurance would be limited to 4% of salary—and yes, if one works in America—from the POTUS on down—they would be required to be a policy holder. It is US, helping out our neighbor...

In picking up on 'why on Earth didn't we do this years ago'—we have had on the books, since 1978 [15 USC § 3101, commonly known as Humphrey-Hawkins], the "legal authorization" to create a "reservoir of public employment" anytime our unemployment rate rises above "3%"....

And to complete the legal mechanism, above, our Social Insurance fund would be triggered anytime our unemployment rate in America, would so rise above 3%....

To put this in context, we have been three times over this percent during far too much of the Great Recession—and we are currently over twice this percent, as I write, as we inch along-- year after year, in a sluggish recovery, i.e., the inevitable result of the path we are currently on—and without getting too cyncial—with one foot still on the plantation [more on this shortly].....

And while, so it seems, the mind automatically defaults to: This is about a liberal social safety net---NTN is, in fact, a Pro-Market concept—and a critical next step in our capitalist economic evolution, i.e., NTN is *Indispensable* to the *Effective* functioning of our 21st Century market economy…and it won't add a dime to our deficit…..

Also, in fairness regarding our dragging our feet in implementation—we do have a lone Congressman, Conyers who periodically introduces legislation to enforce the "legal authorization" in Humphrey-Hawkins, HR 870 and currently HR 1000—to name two—but the black-hearted radical Republicans who currently dominate the House [and also shooting themselves in the foot], will not allow these Bills out of Committee….

And it cannot be stressed strongly enough: This is a Pro-Market concept, based on pragmatism….I am a capitalist, so please spare dragging out "literal" vs "critical" thinking—too much time has already been wasted on nonsense, i.e., communism, socialism lunacy [and without getting too elitist…better liberal, than literal—with the latter not thinking at all]….

For some background, in 1960, our market-driven economies [currently 34 countries]--around the globe joined together given their common market objectives--the Organization for Economic Co-operation and Development, and commonly referred to as OECD.

For the most part the OECD got it right on the money in strengthening the market economy concept....regarding unemployment, however, and to this day, they have it dead wrong....they keep looking to the market to do something it is _incapable_ of doing.....i.e., create enough jobs......

That is, their policy makers, including the U.S., cling to the belief: "The market can provide anybody wanting a job, with a job"—when, in fact, this has _never_ been true—with our Welfare system, alone, in America as empirical evidence Exhibit One....with the result....

"High and persistent unemployment has pervaded almost every OECD country since the mid-1970's.", as reported by internationally recognized Economist, Dr. William F. Mitchell, with double-digit, i.e., 12.6% unemployment common in the Eurozone, and Greece and Spain both in excess of 25%, as I write.....

The major paradigm shift in the world economy in the mid-1970's is explored in detail in the chapters below, but given "automation", alone, NTN, or like programs such as HR 1000, are critical, and indispensable, in solving our joblessness going forward in the 21st Century [Source: Common Sense].....

As reported by ABC News on July 1, 2014 "Eurozone Unemployment Remains High as Economy Lags" .....which is precisely the point of this book, and proposed NTN---

High Unemployment/Sluggish Recovery is not a non-sequitur—people do not buy stuff when they are jobless—It is not smart business—it is anti-capitalism to not fix unemployment—*IMMEDIATELY....yesterday is not soon enough*!

And for a real-time example, here is a truth...Detroit is a ghost town, comparatively....a nightmare, because Washington does not know how to solve our unemployment crisis.....Detroit may be past the point of no return....the jury is still out—but the purpose of this book is to illuminate the path we should be on…..

And it is obvious based on the empirical evidence, alone, that our policy makers in the OECD don't have a clue how to end their/our unemployment crisis…..

A parting thought…..we should never condemn the CEO for closing a plant, when they are losing money….but we should be outraged by policy makers who lack the social/business acumen to address this lapse in a market economy.

In closing out the Prologue, it is transparent that NTN can easily get snarled up in an ideologue sink hole….we humans have a penchant to do that….slap a label on a yet to be employed solution….perhaps, so we don't have to expend any brain power in our evaluation, or for what ever….and even more so in today's pugilistic political climate….

But for absolute clarity---there is _no_ ideologue agenda….the _sole purpose_ is pragmatic—is solely about problem-solving—i.e., to address two extremely serious, and inter-locking social problems going forward in the 21st Century:

Unemployment and the resulting damage
to our Market economy, as a result.

Closing out with a law I crafted—--for our
friends in Economics, in academe:

3% is the zero-sum threshold above which
unemployment triggers inflation by
diminishing labor training and skills,
under-utilizing capital resources, reducing
the rate of productivity advance,
increasing unit labor costs, and reducing
the general supply of goods and services--
and the loss in income to the Market is
compounded exponentially with each
percentage point of increase in
unemployment, above 3%.

Short Definition:

3% is the zero-sum threshold above which
unemployment starts substantially undermining
the Market--and the loss in income to the
Market is compounded exponentially with each
percentage point of increase in unemployment,
above 3%.

Dr. Mitchell closes his daily Blog on Modern Monetary Theory, with "That is enough for today."...and will close out this part of the Prologue with the same, and let the Chapters, below, fill in any blank spots...and agree or disagree, hopefully the offering, here, will have clarity....THX".

CHAPTER SEVEN

President Obama/Council of Economic Advisers:

The late Peter Drucker advocated that no CEO's salary should be greater than 20 times that of their lowest paid employee.

Switzerland recently expanded on this concept, but would limit the CEO's salary to no more than 12 times that of the lowest paid employee.

Naysayers waved and flailed their arms in objection under the "free market" concept, claiming that a CEO's salary should be solely the province of the Market, i.e., determined by the Market, and that artificially setting a CEO's salary would result in a "brain-drain"—which also assumes, among other things, that a CEO would always opt for the higher salary….[is driven solely by GREED]….

And, of course, given that it became law, as proposed by Switzerland—i.e., theoretically universal law—where would they go?

The larger point, here, is the "free market" concept—i.e., what we currently "believe", is solely the province of the Market [sacred ground]—even when this "belief" is detrimental to the Market….

For instance, the most pernicious belief in America, today--indeed, throughout the OECD is the belief that:

"The market can provide anybody wanting a job, with a job"….

For one, this has never been true [with our Welfare system in America, alone, as consummate proof]….

But since the mid-1970's, when the world economy underwent a major paradigm shift— the Market has been less and less capable of creating enough jobs—

And given "automation", alone—going forward into the 21st Century the Market creating enough jobs is becoming exponentially less and less true, daily….

And yet, to this day, our policy makers stand on one foot and then the other….as year after year goes by in a resulting sluggish recovery—entrenched in the "belief" that the Market will create all the jobs we need…..if we just wait long enough…..[and based on a specious "free market" argument]…..

Also ignored, is that the Market thrives when we have a robust, employed, consuming workforce….

The over-arching point is that the Market is INCAPABLE of creating enough jobs in our 21st Century economy—and the "belief", above, is preventing us from finding a solution to pervasive unemployment in America.

Please see Pro-Market, deficit-neutral: HR 1000/THE NEIGHBOR-TO-NEIGHBOR JOB CREATION ACT, Amazon/Kindle

Jim Green, Democrat opponent to Lamar Smith, Congress, 2000

CHAPTER EIGHT

President Obama/Council of Economic Advisers:

ENDING OUR UNEMPLOYMENT CRISIS, IN AMERICA, TOMORROW

As a result of a major paradigm shift in the world economy in the mid-1970's, resulting from automation, globalization, technology, etc., reaching a critical mass [an adjustment towards modernity]--"High and persistent unemployment has pervaded almost every OECD country since the mid-1970's" [Dr. William F. Mitchell]. And given automation, alone, this "social" problem, i.e., pervasive unemployment, will become more and more pronounced with each passing year as we advance into the 21st Century.

Further, in the intervening years since-- Americans have been asserting, louder and louder that "anybody wanting to work should be able to find a job" [86% of Americans believe this—the premise asserted, here, has solid political support]. Indeed, the number one issue in the 2008 election was "Fix Unemployment".

Our means to solve our insidious unemployment crisis, however, and in spite of the paradigm shift, above—our job creation methodology has remained unchanged, i.e., is based on the pernicious belief, and erroneous neo-liberalism propaganda that "the market can provide anybody wanting a job, with a job" with the result:

The CBO projects that it will be 2017, before we return to even an anemic 5.5% unemployment rate, as we inch along—with unemployment benefits long since expired…and if the market fails in the interim, the unemployed are out of luck….

In short, our current job creation is framed around--Fix the market, and this will in turn fix unemployment, when the exact opposite is the path we should be on….i.e., Fix Unemployment, and this will fix the market.

And the irony is that we have the legal "authorization", on the books, to reduce our unemployment rate to 3%, or less, tomorrow, i.e., at no time should our unemployment exceed 3%.

Specifically, As a result of the "malaise", caused by the major paradigm shift, above, the U.S. took an aggressive, pro-active role in addressing this economic shift—and in 1978 President Carter signed into law one of the most important laws in the 20th Century--an expansion of President Truman's [FULL] EMPLOYMENT ACT OF 1946, i.e., Pro-Market 15 USC § 3101--which "authorizes" the creation of a "reservoir of public employees" at any time our unemployment rate in America exceeds "3%"—

Further: "3% is the zero-sum threshold above which unemployment triggers inflation by diminishing labor training and skills, under-utilizing capital resources, reducing the rate of productivity advance, increasing unit labor costs, and reducing the general supply of goods and services--and the loss in income to the Market is compounded exponentially with each percentage point of increase in unemployment, above 3%" [Ending unemployment is a Pro-Market solution].

To address the above, the following is proposed:

1] Codification of The Buffer Stock Employment Model [exported from Australia]: An expanding and contracting public workforce—that expands during a downturn in the market, and contracts as employees return to the private sector—i.e., to maintain our unemployment at 3%, or less—and triggered by the "authorization" in 15 USC § 3101. [and not the least because it is an INDISPENSABLE component in the EFFECTIVE functioning of our 21st Century economy].

2] Passage of the following proposed legislation:

THE NEIGHBOR-TO-NEIGHBOR JOB CREATION ACT

A Pro-Market, deficit-neutral, federally mandated, Social Insurance, owned by our employed, to provide a fund to hire/train our unemployed [with a policy cost limited to 4% of salary].

SECTION 1. SHORT TITLE.

> This Act shall be cited as The Neighbor-To-Neighbor Job Creation Act [To establish employment/training opportunities for the unemployed in compliance with the "Legal Authorization"

in Public Law 15 USC § 3101, for the creation of a "reservoir of public employees", anytime our unemployment rate exceeds "3%", with an emphasis on training for market needs, including a training stipend, where there is a shortage of trained workers--hereafter NTN].

SEC. 2. DEFINITIONS.

In this Act the following definitions apply:

(1) SECRETARY- The term `Secretary' means the Secretary of Labor.
(2) STATE- The term `State' has the meaning given such term in section 102(2) of the Housing and Community Development Act (42 U.S.C. 5302(2)).
(3) TRUST FUND- The term `Trust Fund' refers to the Department of Labor Full Employment Trust Fund.
(4) UNIT OF GENERAL LOCAL GOVERNMENT- The term `unit of general local government' has the meaning given such term in section 102(1) of the Housing and Community Development Act (42 U.S.C. 5302(1)).

(5) URBAN COUNTY- The term `urban county' has the meaning given such term in section 102(6) of the Housing and Community Development Act (42 U.S.C. 5302(6)).

(6) WEB SITE- The Secretary shall establish an internet web site to serve as an information clearinghouse for job training and employment opportunities funded by the Trust Fund.

SEC. 3. EMPLOYMENT OPPORTUNITY GRANTS TO STATES, LOCAL GOVERNMENT.

(a) Use of Funds-A recipient of a grant under this section shall use the grant primarily for infrastructure repair, including, but not limited to:

(A) The painting and repair of schools, community centers, and libraries.

(B) The restoration and revitalization of abandoned and vacant properties to alleviate blight in distressed and foreclosure-affected areas of a unit of general local government.

(C) The augmentation of staffing in Head Start, child care, and other early childhood education programs to promote school readiness and early literacy.

(D) The renovation and enhancement of maintenance of parks, playgrounds, and other public spaces.

[the passage of this single Act, alone, will create more "private-sector" jobs in 6 months, than our current path [HR 2847], in 6 years].

3] Fundamental in framing this model:

1] It is based on the premise that we have far more work that needs to be done in America, than persons to fill these jobs.

2] It must have renewable funding ["jump-start" funding--waiting on the market to kick in" is unworkable, in our 21st Century market economy].

3] It must be deficit-neutral.

In sum, the above is a "win-win" solution: The jobless win, and the Market wins….

FULL EMPLOYMENT IS A PRO-MARKET CONCEPT & WINNERS WANT OTHERS TO WIN, Amazon/Kindle

/S/ Jim Green, Democrat candidate for Congress, District 21, TX, 2000

CHAPTER NINE

President Obama/Council of Economic
Advisers:

Every time a person becomes unemployed, it
cuts into corporate profits....but this is not on
the table....and when we multiply this by 11
million, in the aggregate it is an extremely
serious problem for corporate America,
regarding the bottom line....

Better yet, WHY is this not on the table?

When we speak of our jobless, we speak of their
plight—and that is in no sense diminished by
our looking at the other side of this equation—

Unemployment is a "social" problem, with oft
dire social consequences, we as a society have
the responsibility to address.

To get the oligarchy/plutocracy on board,
however, we need to change the dialogue—we
need to change the message TO: The loss in
corporate profits resulting from
unemployment—which, given automation,

alone, grows exponentially as we advance into the 21ˢᵗ Century:

> "3% is the zero-sum threshold above which unemployment starts substantially undermining the Market--and the loss in income to the Market is compounded exponentially with each percentage point of increase in unemployment, above 3%".

Currently, many in the oligarchy/plutocracy still have one foot on the plantation, cling to the erroneous belief that they need "a pool of slaves" to be used and discarded "at will" [the current status of employment law in America—which they wrote]—and promote the pernicious lie that "The market can provide that the market can provide anybody wanting a job, with a job"---but this mind-set is cutting off their nose to spite their face in the process—

Thus, how do we change the dialogue—how do we build consensus to repair our unemployment crisis?

Consider the following analogy:

30 years ago gays getting married was on no one's radar—it simply wasn't discussed.

Perhaps it started with a single couple who saw this as a right—but in the years since the consensus grew and currently the majority of Americans believe gays should have the right to marry.

And the point is that the same dynamic could be applied in our economic evolution re the unemployed.

The bottom line is, Humphrey-Hawkins [15 USC § 3101] was ahead of its time—when it was signed into law in 1978, by President Carter—Now it is Indispensable to the Effective functioning of our 21st Century market economy....

And, the over-arching point is that until we change the dialogue--change the message--we are not going to solve our insidious unemployment crisis in America.

FULL EMPLOYMENT IS A PRO-MARKET CONCEPT, Amazon

Jim Green, Democrat opponent to Lamar Smith, Congress, 2000

CHAPTER TEN

President Obama/Council of Economic Advisers:

It is like a dark family secret….like a crazy aunt that everyone in the family knows about….but never talks about:

The vacuum that surrounds a persons rights when we go to work in America…..we all know about it—and unwittingly participate in our ceasing to be an American citizen when we go to work…

Dr. David Ewing, in his book "Freedom Inside The Organiztion" defined it this way….

"Employee rights are like a Black Hole in space, so impacted by tradition that light can barely escape.".

A truism is that a slave is a person without rights, by definition….and our employment laws in America still have one foot on the plantation--
-

And the sad reality is the "belief" that we need A POOL OF SLAVES: To Be Used and Discarded "at will" [Amazon]…. a concept that worked poorly in the 20th Century, and not at all in our 21st Century economy—and creates horrid results…..

And a consummate illustration is the Hobby Lobby case recently before the SCUS, in which the Court allowed a corporation "personhood"—[a status that has taken on a bizarre definition by the anti-choice folk]—so that the "corporation" has control over women's reproductive rights…[where it should have NONE]!

But the mother of all our "slave labor" laws--are our "Right To Work" laws—which started making their rounds in the various states [much like the ALEC laws, today] in the 1950's—and a misnomer if one ever existed!

Speciously offered as an effort to strengthen the rights of the employee—in fact, the intent [to this day] is a cynical abuse of employee rights—i.e., the objective is the systematic destruction of unions—with the resulting pernicious destruction of a strong middle class in America!

There is an adage: "Never follow a trend out a window"….and the point, here, is that our turning a blind eye to the systematic destruction of employee rights over the past 100 years [one step forward, two back] has a destructive effect on job creation in our 21st Century economy—and on our economy, itself—high unemployment/sluggish recovery is not a non-sequitur.

The over-arching point, here, is that while we unwittingly cling to this archaic mind-set—It has taken us 180 degrees off course in job creation, in our 21st Century economy, and has caused unwarranted damage to the Market in the process!

HR 1000/THE NEIGHBOR-TO-NEIGHBOR JOB CREATION ACT, Amazon

Jim Green, Democrat opponent to Lamar Smith, 2000

CHAPTER ELEVEN

President Obama/Council of Economic Advisers/Fellow Democrats:

OUR RECOVERY INCHES ALONG DRAGGING A SACRED COW:

"Most [Americans think] that anybody willing to work should be able to find a job….". Indeed, a Zogby Poll found that 86% of Americans think this.

AND, we have the LEGAL AUTHORITY, on the books, to make this a reality in Public Law 15 USC § 3101—a deficit-neutral, Pro-Market means to address the wishes of the American people [see below]….

So why do we have 11.3 million unemployed Americans, and a 6.2% unemployment rate [quadruple for minority youth]?

We are a democracy…under our Constitution the government serves at the will of the American people….

Under the Public Law, above, there is no time in which our unemployment rate in America should exceed 3%....

SO WHAT IS CAUSING THIS CHASM BETWEEN PUBLIC WILL, AND POLICY IN WASHINGTON?

And, virtually every policy maker in Washington must share the blame by default....

In looking for a solution to our unemployment crisis in America, they almost universally default to the anachronistic and totally unworkable belief in a modern market economy—a SACRED COW:

THE BELIEF that the market can provide everyone wanting a job, with a job [and if the market fails, the unemployed are out of luck]....

And yet, the market has been less and less capable of creating enough jobs—given automation, technology, globalization, etc., since the mid-1970's—with pervasive high and persistent unemployment in most of the OECD countries since that time...

It appears, our policy makers celebrate automation and then get "a deer in the headlights" regarding the displaced worker—and the adverse "social" consequences of unemployment.

As a result our policies have been framed around: Fix the market, and this will fix unemployment—when our framework should be exactly the opposite: Fix unemployment, and this will fix the market.

FIXING UNEMPLOYMENT IS ANTITHETICAL TO THE OBJECTIVE OF THE MARKET—IT ISN'T WHAT THEY DO.....

Proposed, here, is deficit-neutral/Pro-Market **THE NEIGHBOR-TO-NEIGHBOR JOB CREATION ACT: A federally mandated Social Insurance, owned by our employed, to provide a fund to hire/train our unemployed. For a modest 4% of salary policy cost we can reduce our unemployment to 3% within a year—and this will create more "private-sector" jobs in 6 months, than our current path [HR 2847] in 6 years.**

HR 870/FULL EMPLOYMENT IS A PRO-MARKET CONCEPT/ IT IS IMPOSSIBLE TO BE A CHRISTIAN, AND VOTE REPUBLICAN Amazon/Kindle

Jim Green, Democrat opponent to Lamar Smith, Congress, 2000

CHAPTER TWELVE

President Obama/Council of Economic
Advisers:

RE: LAYING the FOUNDATION for
RECOVERY & GROWTH

President Obama had a weapon in addressing
our economic meltdown in 2008, in America—
not available to FDR during the Great
Depression:

And this was the billions from Military
Retirement and Social Security Insurance
percolating up through our economy—

In short, were it not for these moneys we would
not be talking about having narrowly averted
another Great Depression—we would be buried
in one!

Also, this model is a "win-win"—it addresses a
critical social need, as well as benefits the
economy i.e., the market—and yet the
Republicans want to tamper with this vibrant
social benefit in their short-sighted agenda to

pander to the GREED of the 1%--it is their One and Only program!

In short, this model is a "pro-market" concept—and least understood: An INDISPENSABLE component to the proper functioning of the market going forward in the 21st Century—

The market thrives when we have a robust, employed, consuming workforce—but given the proliferating volatile nature of the market [the obsolete cycle is getting shorter and shorter], _the market is no longer capable of producing the jobs necessary to its viability_—and it is essential that we address this void with public sector jobs—ON BEHALF OF THE MARKET!

> The Buffer Stock Employment Model--an expanding and contracting public workforce—that expands during downturns in the market, and contracts as employees return to the private-sector—[in theory, triggered under Public Law 15 USC § 3101, anytime our jobless rate rises above 3%] was introduced at the University of Chicago in 1998, by Dr. William Mitchell, signaled a solution to this economic dilemma facing a modern market economy: Fix the market and this will fix

our unemployment crisis vs fix unemployment and this will in turn fix the market—[

"Conventional Wisdom", to date, has exclusively taken the former path—and the result has been a disaster—and in spite of a 6.3% unemployment rate—we still have 12 million jobless Americans, a sluggish recovery—and a CBO projection of 5 years just to get back to 5.5%--with unemployment benefits long since expired!

Proposed, here, is The Neighbor-To-Neighbor Job Creation Act: A federally mandated mutual insurance, owned by our employed, to provide a fund to hire/train our unemployed. For a modest policy cost of 4% of salary we can reduce our unemployment to 3%, within a year of passage, and as "authorized" under Public Law 15 USC § 3101. The lone legislation in Washington, at present, relevant to the above is HR 1000 [currently in Committee].

See also, "OUR GREED AND IGNORANCE" on Amazon/Kindle; www.Inclusivism.org .

Jim Green, Democrat candidate for Congress, 2000

CHAPTER THIRTEEN

President Obama/Council of Economic Advisers:

As a delegate to the Texas Democrat Convention this past week, I asked two questions in meetings, in bars, just about anywhere fellow Democrats wanted to jawbone:

1] FULL EMPLOYMENT IS A PRO-MARKET CONCEPT [not coincidentally also the title of a book I have on Amazon—but hang out]....and then I would add [with universal agreement]: Common sense, right—people do not buy stuff when they are jobless, right.....And here is the hammer this setup was leading to:

So why isn't it a fact?

It is our $64,000 question, today, and begs the question [in support of the market, alone] why is it not being asked daily, or hourly in Washington—

We are, in theory, a democracy, so when 86% of Americans believe that "anybody wanting to work should be able to find a job"--EVERY effort should me made to make this a fact—

When, in fact, NO effort is being made in Washington to make this a fact—[lip service, no laws] which raises the additional question are we, in fact, an oligarchy as recent studies suggest? Is this why 50% of Americans don't vote?

The other side of this coin is that people not buying stuff undermines the market....our disappearing manufacturing base is not totally due to our jobs going to the Far East....

With the current result a "no one wins"—the jobless lose, and the Market loses...

Which leads to the second question asked of my Compadres:

2] *Do you believe the market can provide anybody wanting a job, with a job?*

And this is the universal catch-all that undermines our solving the first question asked—We don't look for a solution when we BELIEVE we have one.....

And thus we stand on one foot and then the other waiting on the market to provide our jobs—with the CBO projecting it will be 2017 for us to get back to even an anemic 5.5% jobless rate--

When the truth is the market has NEVER been able to provide everybody with a job…with our Welfare system empirical Exhibit ONE--And given "automation" alone, going forward—this pernicious BELIEF becomes exponentially less viable, almost daily!

In sum, Humphrey-Hawkins [15 USC § 3101] was ahead of its time—when it was signed into law in 1978, by President Carter—Now it is Indispensable to the Effective functioning of our 21st Century economy--RE: HR 1000/The Neighbor-To-Neighbor Job Creation Act

Jim Green, Democrat opponent to Lamar Smith, Congress, 2000

CHAPTER FOURTEEN

President Obama/Council of Economic Advisers:

Capitalism is ideal in producing and selling corn flakes and cars—It doesn't work in solving "social problems" such as unemployment and our healthcare....

And when we have tried "privatization" to solve our social problems—it has been a disaster:

Essential programs have been cut—such as the elimination of text books from the Job Corps education program—to increase profits, and cronyism has been rampant—

And in our "for profit" healthcare system, billions of dollars are siphoned away from the premiums we send in—and do not go to the healthcare of ANYONE—but rather is used to pay for lobbyists, to make the CEO's filthy rich—and spent on propaganda ads to keep it that way!

Further, it attracts a few who see healthcare as a means to get rich, rather than cure the ill....

The truth is, we currently have a blended system—and they are, in fact, indispensable to each other:

Were it not for Social Security Insurance moneys percolating up through our economy in 2008—we would not be talking about having narrowly averted another Great Depression—We would be buried in one!

Social Insurance is a vital ingredient in building a vibrant and decent society—And, invent a better widget, sell the company for a million bucks, and retire in South Florida [capitalism]—is as well a vital ingredient in building a vibrant and decent society.

So why do we have this war of words pitting the two against each other—rather than educating the American people regarding the indispensable symbiotic relationship they have to each other?

Most Republicans ask God in their prayers at night to be protected from becoming communists, or socialists, or even worse "liberals"—

And this war of words disguises that the Republican Party, today, is not the Pro-Market party they boast—but rather their policies are, in fact, Anti-Market—destructive to capitalism!

Pandering to the GREED of their wealthiest contributors—the Republican One and Only program—is NOT a Pro-Market concept!

Another misnomer in the war of words, is right-wing invented "entitlement"—a word that should be banned from honest discussion—do we refer to our auto insurance as an "entitlement"?

And when Social Security Insurance brings in more that it pays out, i.e., is deficit-neutral--how is that an "entitlement", and why is it portrayed in our graphs as a "government expense"—or even included in these graphs? If a corporation reported a massive loss on a product they in fact made money—they would be charged with fraud in a New York Minute!

The list goes on—please see: OUR GREED AND IGNORANCE, on Amazon/Kindle

Jim Green, Democrat congressional opponent to Lamar Smith, 2000

CHAPTER FIFTEEN

FAIL-SAFE ELECTRONIC VOTING

TO THE READER: Given you have gotten this far, and agree with the proposed changes—and particularly given the pernicious Citizens United—our democracy, and the above, or any, progress, will be in peril absent a "fail-safe" electronic voting system. The following is my proposed solution, and like every solution proposed, here, feed-back--your proposed improvement, etc. is welcomed:

THE FAIL-SAFE ELECTRONIC VOTING ACT

1) EVERY electronic voting machine (hereafter EVM), must be inexpensive, identical throughout the U.S. in a 1/150 ratio, and *must count and produce a hard-copy of the recorded votes.* In addition, an extra copy of their recorded votes would be produced (not necessarily a hard-copy), marked "Voter's Copy", and containing "NOTICE: Do Not Destroy Until Every Election On Your Ballot Is Certified". [If Wal-Mart handed us a piece of

paper with the words "trust us" as a receipt for our purchases—we would be outraged—and yet, this is our current electronic voting nightmare—but in this case it is our democracy at risk]!

2) *After confirming that their votes are recorded correctly*, the voter would then insert the hard-copy ballot into a software-free (count only) optical scanner (hereafter OS), for a second count. The hard-copy ballot would be retained by election officials in the event a candidate asks for a recount (*not possible under the current system, and which undermines the legality of each such election*). The EVM and the OS must be manufactured by different companies (which is universally true today).

3) Election officials assigned to oversee the EVM, would be prevented by law from overseeing the OS, and vice-versa, and stiff criminal penalties would be imposed for violations.

4) Further, every EVM would be programmed with raw data re the total registration rolls, by party, and norms for their voting history, etc.,---as an "alert" to a possible irregularity, such as an "under-vote"—or "vote-flipping" etc., and *standards* established to suspend certification

where there is an "improbable result", at least temporarily, of a particular election until the discrepancy is cleared up. (This is what computers do best, and it would be very easy to create such a program).

5) At the end of the election day, tallies would be taken from the EVM and the OS, for each candidate. *If the tallies didn't balance for any given election, or if there is an "alert", that election cannot be certified until the "error" is corrected.* If the candidates agree (the victory is certain), minor discrepancies in the count could be disregarded. While probably rare, the Voter, or a random sample of Voters, would be required by law to return their Copy of the recorded votes to the election office to clear up any "error", or where an "alert" signals the need for same.

6) Further, every state provides for a recount when the total vote falls below a certain percent of difference between the candidates, impossible to conduct with the current EVM. And thus Congress must mandate the following regarding presidential candidates: A RUN-OFF election is mandated and triggered in those states where the percent of total vote is less than .5% of difference between the two candidates; said

election to be held on the second Saturday following the election, on PAPER BALLOTS ONLY, and contain ONLY the names of the relevant candidates, for instance: "Barack Obama, Democrat" and "John McCain, Republican"—with oversight in counting by a representative(s) of each party—said procedure providing more than adequate time to meet the Electoral College mandate [Ideally, all of this could be eliminated if we did away with the Electoral College, but until then....]. NOTE: Had this been the law in 2000, Al Gore would be our president, and America would have been spared the economic, etc., disaster that followed!

7) Finally, absent the above safeguards, and until these safeguards are in place--Congress must mandate that PAPER BALLOTS, ONLY, can be used in our presidential elections. This is not a "partisan" issue, it is a "pro-democracy" issue. Most importantly, this will return the responsibility for our elections, and our vote counting, back into the hands of the individual voter, where it belongs, and out of the hands of "corporate control"---*it is* after all "our democracy", itself, that is at risk if we don't take these steps---and in that regard, is there any time or cost differential that is too great?

Jim Green

CHAPTER SIXTEEN

I didn't write the following. It is a cut and paste from FACEBOOK, or some blog [would like to give credit if knew the author]--but it is so on target regarding how "fear" is driving Conservative policy in America today—i.e., is undermining America and our progress—and relegating America to a Third World country status, rather than a world leader—FDR had it on the nose in "All we have to fear, is fear itself"…at his inaugural in 1933….

"Conservatives are such cowards: they are afraid of gay people getting married or serving in the military; they are afraid of bringing terrorists to super max prisons in the US from which no one has ever escaped; they are afraid of the boy scouts letting gay kids in; they are afraid of everyone voting and are constantly suppressing the vote under some bogus voter fraud theory; they are afraid of letting students vote at their universities; they are afraid of women having the right to choose; they even are afraid of women getting contraception [the real issue actually is a women's agency and control over their bodies]; they are afraid of immigration reform leading to citizenship because they are afraid of-- name whatever reason; they are afraid of mandating gun purchasers to undergo background checks for crazy people and terrorists; they are afraid of people smoking pot; they are afraid of climate change being real and contradicting their beloved Bible; they are afraid of legitimate campaign reform; they are afraid of Muslims; they are afraid of blacks; they are afraid of atheists; they are afraid of hippies; they are afraid of socialists; they are probably still afraid of monsters under their beds; they are just rank cowards and keep making things up to be afraid of."

CHAPTER SEVENTEEN

[I couldn't resist including this…and yes I am the author…..]

A MESSAGE FROM GOD

MANY CENTURIES AGO, a man of the cloth, we don't know his name, and in a flash of insight (perhaps induced by peyote) told his flock that "sex is a sin". And lo and behold he learned that by taking a very natural and healthy part of our life and turning it into something that was "dirty and nasty", that he could imprison his flock, and fill his coffers, and hallelujah it was a great day for the Lord!

Quickly, his miracle spread to other churches in his village, and then to the next village, and then the next county, and then state, and soon it spread to all the churches in the ancient world, and all of their flocks cowed in fear and shame and became imprisoned, and their coffers over-floweth. Hallelujah, it was a great day for the Lord!

And to keep the myth alive they started inventing stories, half-baked stories, that made no sense to anyone who is rational, such as "Mary was a virgin"—well, she just had to be a virgin because she would never partake in anything that was dirty and nasty, like sex (if you're doing it right), and this was necessary to make "sex is a sin" make sense...so they invented a Mary that was "sinless"--you get the picture. And their coffers over-floweth. Hallelujah, it was a great day for the Lord!

No one seemed to be bothered that when we play tricks on the human mind by taking something that is very natural and healthy, such as sex, and make it dirty and nasty that all kind of bad things happen to the human mind:

Such as most pedophiles, and most serial killers, and voting Republican, and unwarranted suicides, and most mental illness, and unwanted pregnancies. (Teens not wanting to have sex is the perversion, not the other way around, and by replacing sex education and condoms, with unrealistic "abstinence", and by using blather about "low self-esteem" to shame them into not "sinning"—We have a teen pregnancy in the U.S. twice that of England and Canada!).

But none of this mattered, because their coffers over-floweth, and Hallelujah, it is a great day for the Lord!

There is a cure--------Tell these right-wing loonies to shove it....

GOD

ABOUT THE AUTHOR: I was employed in our Criminal Justice System for a cumulative 20 years as a probation officer, with 5 of those years as a chief probation officer. I authored the concept of "Shock Incarceration" which became law in Kansas in 1970, and then was adopted in numerous jurisdictions in the U.S. and also spread to Europe—it is currently identified in the U.S. as "Boot Camp" [as the means to "shock" the young offender—and a total distortion of my original intent—like many ideas, once released, they take on a life of their own]. I also instigated establishment of the first Court Psychiatric Clinic in the U.S., in conjunction with psychiatrists from the Menninger Foundation, as a chief probation officer. Finally, I was the Democrat candidate for Congress, District 21, TX, 2000. I would most define myself as a Social Ecologist-- [albeit my degree is in Psychology]. My web page is www.Inclusivism.org –which has been on the internet since 1996.

A BRIEF ADDENDUM: When the U.S. Supreme Court denied certiorari—where the violation of my constitutional rights were obvious, and criminal negligence on the part of the government defendants in the death of our son, equally obvious—[detailed in THE HARVARD BOYS CLUB, Amazon/Kindle]--I filed a Petition for Rehearing [which is automatic]—and included the following. The Clerk of the U.S. Supreme Court called me at my work in California, and asked that I withdraw the "cartoon" [a reprint from The NEW YORKER] from my Petition. I refused on the basis of the First Amendment, and it remains in the archives at the U.S. Supreme Court [Docket #: 79-1627], to this day. The wording [not that clear] is: "Excellent, excellent. A fine blend of truths, half-truths, and blatant falsehoods".

IN THE

Supreme Court of the United States

October Term, 1979

No. 79-1627

JAMES L. GREEN,

Petitioner,

vs.

And others: http://www.amazon.com/James-L.-Jim-Green/e/B001KHZIMM/ref=ntt_dp_epwbk_0

www.ingramcontent.com/pod-product-compliance
Lightning Source LLC
Chambersburg PA
CBHW060200290526
45789CB00003B/1097